A city adventure in ...

Sydney

by Amy Allatson

Words in yellow can be found in the glossary on page 24.

Contents

Page 4   What is a City?

Page 6   Where is Sydney?

Page 8   Where and Why?

Page 10   Sightseeing in Sydney

Page 12   Food in Sydney

Page 14   Travelling Around Sydney

Page 16   Where do People Live in Sydney?

Page 18   Geography

Page 20   Out and About

Page 22   What is It?

Page 23   Quick Quiz

Page 24   Glossary and Index

©2017
Book Life
King's Lynn
Norfolk PE30 4LS

ISBN: 978-1-78637-053-2

Printed in Malaysia

A catalogue record for this book is available from the British Library.

Written by:
Amy Allatson

Edited by:
Charlie Ogden

Designed by:
Ian McMullen

What is a City?

Cities are urban settlements. They are bigger in size than towns and villages and have larger populations. Cities are usually very busy places with lots of buildings.

In every country there are cities and most countries have a capital city. Cities are usually home to many people from different cultures.

WHAT IS A CAPITAL CITY?
A capital city is usually home to a country's government.

Where is Sydney?

Sydney is one of Australia's largest cities and is located on the east coast of Australia. To the south of Sydney is Australia's capital city, Canberra, and to the north is another city, Brisbane.

Population: Over 4.2 million

Famous building: Sydney Opera House

Language: English

Coldest months: June and July

Average temperature: 15°C

Warmest months: December to February

Average temperature: 30°C

Darwin
Brisbane
Alice Springs
Perth
Sydney
Canberra

Flight No.

AM A24-11-88-9

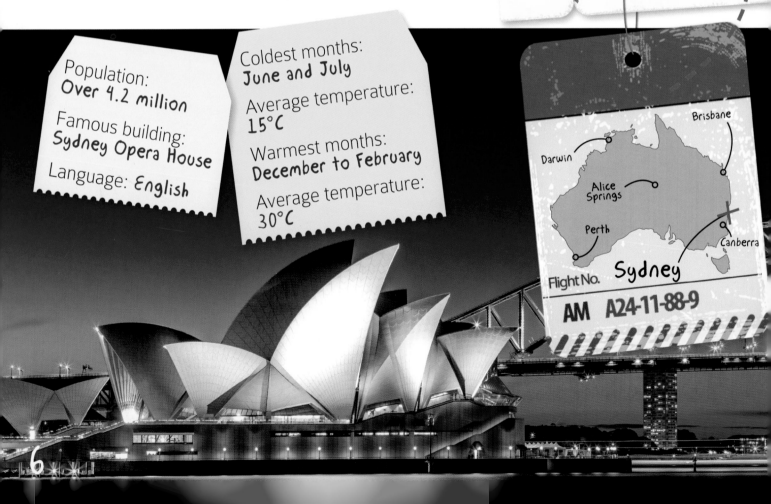

8599IZ

Bondi Beach in Sydney

Over 30 million tourists visit Sydney every year for its warm climate and long stretches of sandy beach.

Where and Why?

Captain James Cook

The land Sydney is built upon was home to Aboriginal Australians for many years before it was discovered by the English explorer Captain James Cook.

England sent convicts to Sydney over 200 years ago to help build settlements that could house more convicts. The city grew and grew until it became as large and busy as it is today.

Sightseeing in Sydney

Koala

Kangaroo

FLIGHT NO:

There are lots of things to see and do in Sydney. Tourists can visit the famous Sydney Opera House on the harbour. They can also visit the city zoo to see animals such as kangaroos and koalas.

Tourists can visit one of Sydney's many beaches, such as the famous Bondi Beach, where they can go swimming or learn how to surf.

11

Food in Sydney

Usually Sydney has a warm and sunny climate, so lots of meals are eaten outside. Food is sometimes cooked on a barbecue.

Sometimes people have barbecues on the beach.

Lots of food, such as meat and vegetables, can be cooked on a barbecue. This is done by placing food over burning wood or coals to cook.

Travelling Around Sydney

People can travel around Sydney by tram. A tram is a type of small train that travels around a city on tracks.

A tram travelling around Sydney.

People can also travel around Sydney's harbour by water taxi. Water taxis are a quick and fun way to travel.

Where do People Live in Sydney?

Lots of people in Sydney live in flats in very tall buildings.

Modern flats in Sydney

Some people in Sydney live near to the ocean. This is because it is usually cooler by the ocean and there are lots of things to do on Sydney's many beaches.

Waterfront homes in Sydney

17

Geography

Sydney is built around a harbour. Sydney Harbour is one of the deepest natural harbours in the world, with some parts measuring in at 45 metres deep.

Sydney Opera House

Sydney Harbour contains the Sydney Harbour Bridge, which stands at 141 metres above sea level and is 1,149 metres long.

The Sydney Harbour Bridge is the tallest steel arch bridge in the world.

Out and About

There are lots of things to do out and about in Sydney. There are many parks and gardens around the city to play in and explore.

The Royal Botanic Garden in Sydney.

Although Sydney is mostly flat, on the edge of the city people can visit part of a mountain range called the Blue Mountains.

The Blue Mountains near Sydney

What is It?

Can you write down what's in the pictures below? These are all things that are found in Sydney.

Quick Quiz

1. How many people live in Sydney?

2. Can you name a famous landmark in Sydney?

3. What animals can you see at the zoo?

4. How many metres deep are the deepest parts of Sydney Harbour?

5. How many beaches are there in Sydney?

Glossary

Aboriginal Australians	a group of people who were the first to live in Australia
climate	the weather in an area
convicts	people who have committed a crime
cultures	attitudes and beliefs of a country or a group of people
explorer	a person who discovers a new area
government	a group of people who make a country's rules and laws
harbour	a part of an ocean or lake that is next to land and is deep enough for ships
modern	something from recent or present times
mountain range	a group of connected mountains
populations	the number of people who live in certain places
urban settlements	places where lots of people live and work, like towns or cities

Index

Aboriginal 8
animals 10
beaches 7, 11–12, 17
buildings 4, 6, 16
climates 7, 12

food 12–13
mountains 21
parks 20
populations 4, 6
settlements 4, 9

tourists 7, 10–11,
towns 4
travelling 14–15

Photo Credits

Abbreviations: l-left, r-right, b-bottom, t-top, c-centre, m-middle.
2 – pisaphotography. 4, 13 – CroMary. 5 – Zarya Maxim Alexandrovich 6 – Tooykrub. 7 – Aleksandar Todorovic. 8 – Georgios Kollidas.
8frame – Roman Samokhin. 9 – Triff. 9r – Skoda. 10 – Eric Isselee. 11 – BlueOrange Studio. 12 – Kzenon. 12inset – Beata Becla. 14 –
PomInOz. 15 – Neale Cousland. 16 – Thorsten Rust. 17 – Phillip Minnis. 18-19 – Dan Breckwoldt. 20 – DAE Photo. 21 – Leelakajonkij.
Images are courtesy of Shutterstock.com. With thanks to Getty Images, Thinkstock Photo and iStockphoto.